BRITISH RAIL IN COLOUR No. 2

Compiled by
Hugh Dady

Copyright © Jane's Publishing Company Limited 1987

First published in the United Kingdom in 1987 by
Jane's Publishing Company Limited
238 City Road, London EC1V 2PU

ISBN 0 7106 0430 0

Printed in the United Kingdom
by Netherwood Dalton & Co Ltd, Huddersfield

JANE'S TRANSPORT PRESS

Cover illustrations

Front: No 58030 passes Acton Canal Wharf with 7Z69 Silverhill-
Northfleet mgr working. 16 May 1986. *(Hugh Dady)*
Nikkormat FT2   50mm Nikkor   Kodachrome 64   1/500, f4

Rear: Tailpiece at Paddington; HST power cars are Nos 43142
(nearest), 43180 and 43183. 2 March 1985. *(Hugh Dady)*
Nikkormat FT2   50mm Nikkor   Kodachrome 64   7 sec, f5.6

Right: No 37027 *Loch Eil* near Arieniskill Farm at the western end
of Loch Eilt with the 1005 Fort William–Mallaig. An Stac is the
mountain in the background, prominent from the railway in the
neighbourhood of Lochailort. 21 May 1985. *(Andrew Vines)*
*Bronica ETR-S   75mm Zenzanon   Ektachrome Pro 64
1/250, f6.3*

INTRODUCTION

During 1985 the cans of British Rail blue were pushed to the back of the store as the clamour for new liveries gained momentum. However, it wasn't just the sectors that felt entitled to personalised liveries. Led by the PTEs, various geographical areas sought their own identification, while approval was given for special paint jobs to mark events such as GW150. BR blue is not dead, but it must now share a place with some more exotic shades on the BR colour card. By the spring of 1986 some standardisation had emerged for the new colour schemes. Even so, at the time of writing, there were seven major variants for the Class 47 alone, never mind a host of minor oddities. The railway scene is rapidly brightening up, so the justification for colour photography has become even stronger.

Since the original BR colour albums, many changes have occurred on the motive power front. A new generation of dmus has arrived, though not yet as standardised as BR had led us to believe. Introduction of the Class 58 heavy freight locomotive has been plagued with problems, the APT project is shelved, and for the first time BR is playing host to privately-owned locomotives — and not even British products at that! The future motive power re-equipment programme will be watched with interest as British manufacturers fight it out with competition from across the Atlantic.

The pictures for this volume are drawn mainly from the early 1980s, a period that will be remembered as the last years of a common corporate identity. The new liveries, which began as a trickle, are represented in these pages; future volumes will cover those which at present lie on the drawing board.

As always, Ken Harris at Jane's has provided plenty of encouragement for the project. May I thank all the contributing photographers who collectively have amassed several thousand hours by the lineside in this enjoyable but sometimes frustrating hobby!

HUGH DADY
Ealing
November 1986

Fresh from overhaul, No 31302 hurries the Doncaster works test train north near Woodcroft Crossing on the ECML. 7 December 1985. *(John Rudd)*
Mamiya 645   80mm Mamiya   Agfa R100S   1/250, f5.6

Class 207 (3D) demu No 1303 at Eridge awaiting connections from Uckfield and London, prior to forming the 1257 shuttle to Tonbridge. 11 February 1985.

(Andrew Vines)
Bronica ETR-S   75mm Zenzanon
Ektachrome Pro 100   1/500, f11

On 19 June 1986 No 56037 *Richard Trevithick*, hauling 6Z89, the 1400 Allington-Westbury ARC empties, passes LRT's Lillie Bridge depot at Earl's Court and attempts to race a train of District line stock to Kensington Olympia. After interest generated by the speculative construction of No HS 4000 *Kestrel* in 1967, then the most powerful single-engined ac generation diesel-electric, Brush Electrical Machines had entered into an agreement with its Romanian counterpart Electroputere of Craiova to develop a heavy freight locomotive for Eastern bloc countries. Thus when BRB identified an urgent need in 1973 for such a locomotive to meet an upsurge in coal and heavy freight traffic, a design was already available. The first of 30 units constructed in Romania arrived in 1976; subsequent lots were built at Doncaster and finally Crewe.
(Hugh Dady)
Nikkormat FT2   85mm Nikkor
Kodachrome 64   1/500, f4

Transport costs in the aggregate business represent a major proportion of the final cost. Frustrated by the poor availability of BR locomotives to move its traffic, Foster Yeoman considered the purchase of its own engines. This led to a unique agreement allowing privately-owned locomotives to run over BR lines, albeit crewed and maintained with the help of BR. The Electro-Motive Division of General Motors won the contract for four units, which were designated Class 59 by BR. The locomotives arrived in the UK at the end of January 1986, and after acceptance trials at Derby went straight into service. On 26 March 1986 No 59003 climbs out of Acton yard with the 0858 for Purfleet. *(Hugh Dady)*
Nikkormat FT2   85mm Nikkor
Kodachrome 64   1/500, f4

Above: The reintroduction of Pullman services on the LM and ER during 1985 was a welcome move which demonstrated that customers are willing to pay for a premium service. On 26 May 1986 No 86101 *Sir William A. Stanier FRS* wheels through the Buckinghamshire countryside near Linslade with the 1605 Liverpool-Euston Pullman. The three Class 86/1 locomotives were rebuilt in 1972 with BP9 bogies and spring-borne GEC G412AZ traction motors similar to those fitted to Class 87s. At 5000 hp they are thus the most powerful variant of the 100 Class 86s. *(Hugh Dady)*
Nikkormat FT2   85mm Nikkor
Kodachrome 64   1/500, f3.8

Right: The WCML can boast heavier utilisation than most other main lines but the volume of freight still compares very poorly with continental systems. Just three daytime Speedlink services were booked to leave Willesden for the north during 1986. On 27 May 1986 No 86412 *Elizabeth Garratt Anderson* ambles down the slow lines near Carpenders Park with 6S73, the 1059 Dover Town-Mossend Speedlink. *(Hugh Dady)*
Nikkormat FT2   85mm Nikkor
Kodachrome 64   1/500, f3.5

The sun sinks low at Chinley as No 47469 *Glasgow Chamber of Commerce,* heading the 1520 Glasgow-Nottingham, sweeps through the junction with the single line to Peak Forest. 18 June 1986. *(Les Nixon)*

Pentax 6 × 7 150mm Takumar Ektachrome 64

Under a dramatic sky No 47708 *Waverley* propels a shortened push-pull set towards Plean Junction, en route to the Perth railfare on 13 April 1985. The small stud of Class 47/7s is used almost exclusively on the Glasgow-Edinburgh and Glasgow-Aberdeen push-pull services and these locomotives are permitted to run up to 100 mph, unlike their sister sub-classes, which are limited to 95 mph. The attractive livery was just one aspect of an aggressive marketing policy developed for the Scottish Region under the then General Manager Chris Green. With a new identity as ScotRail, and an enterprising package of improvements achieved with the support of local authorities, the railway has been given a new lease of life. *(W J Verden Anderson) Nikon 85mm Nikkor Kodachrome 64 1/500, f4*

Above: Nos 33118 and 33001 cross Balcombe viaduct with ECS from Clapham yard to form the 0914 Brighton-Penzance on 7 September 1985. The Cromptons had taken over the original Brighton-Exeter service from steam in May 1966, but in October 1971 the train was withdrawn until the following spring when it reappeared as a Saturdays-only train formed with a Hastings demu. Locomotive haulage returned to the service in May 1977, and by the following summer it was back to full strength and requiring a pair of Class 33s. The 1983 timetable saw the service extended to Penzance, with a Class 50 usually taking over the train at Exeter St David's. On summer Saturdays in 1986 the train ran through to Penzance, but for the rest of the year stopped at Exeter. *(Andrew Marshall)*
Minolta SRT 100X   50mm Rokkor
Kodachrome 64   1/250, f4.5

Right: The 1135 Penzance-Plymouth local is an easy proposition for No 50028 *Tiger* crossing Lynher viaduct to the east of St Germans on 16 August 1984. After the initial influx of HSTs to the West Country, locomotives made a comeback during 1984-85 when HSTs were redrafted to routes offering more business potential. With most Class 50s based at Laira their use in the Duchy seems assured, although probably on a reducing scale as HSTs once again become available after the East Coast electrification. *(Andrew Marshall)*
Minolta SRT 100X   50mm Rokkor
Kodachrome 64   1/500, f4

BR's own contender for the medium-weight dmu replacement programme, the Class 150, quickly proved itself. Even before the first unit had been handed over on 8 June 1984, tenders had been invited for a production fleet which the Provincial Services sector quickly dubbed 'Sprinters'. Two prototypes, each with different drive arrangements, were given extensive testing. The first, fitted with Cummins engines and Voith transmission, proved to be the better machine and formed the basis for production units. No 150002, seen here at Milford with a Matlock-Derby service on 13 November 1985, was fitted with Rolls-Royce Eagle C6 280 HR engines driving through Self Changing Gears R500 gearboxes. This second prototype was troublesome in service, and by the summer of 1986 it seemed likely that it would be chosen for conversion to a 90 mph 'Super Sprinter'. *(B S Dean)*
Pentax Super A   100mm Pentax
Fujichrome 100   1/500, f4.5

The Class 151 medium-weight dmu designed and built by Metro-Cammell began evaluation trials in February 1985. It had been intended as an alternative to BR's own Class 150 'Sprinter' unit, but constructional difficulties delayed its introduction. Each car is powered by an underfloor Cummins NT 855-R4 engine similar to that fitted in the first prototype 'Sprinter' unit. The fully-automatic BSI coupler, incorporating mechanical, electrical and pneumatic connections, eliminates the need for unsightly jumper cables. The stylish units are perhaps only slightly marred by the roof humps containing fans and intakes for air circulation in the saloon. During 1985 the two units spent most of their time on the Matlock branch, and this view shows No 151002 approaching Matlock with an afternoon service from Sinfin on 9 August 1985. *(Barrie Walker)*
Leica M2   Kodachrome 25   1/250, f4

On the evening of 3 January 1984 No 50007 *Hercules* was just another member of the Western's exclusive Class 50 fleet waiting to leave Waterloo with the 1910 service to Exeter. Within a few weeks though she was called to Laira where a metamorphosis occurred and the name 'Hercules' disappeared into history (see page 34). The Waterloo-Exeter service requires six locomotives, each working a three-day cycle. At the London end light servicing can be carried out at Stewart's Lane, but any defect of a more serious nature requires the locomotive to make the short journey to Old Oak Common via the West London extension. *(Hugh Dady)*
Nikkormat FT2   50mm Nikkor
Kodachrome 64   5 sec, f4

No shortage of history here — the location is Ipswich, now transformed by electrification. Back in 1980, though, Class 47s held sway on nearly all passenger services. On the evening of 23 September 1980 No 47016 is about to depart with the 1930 Liverpool Street-Yarmouth, while on the right No 47170 *County of Norfolk* patiently awaits the return of Norwich supporters for the 2135 return footex. Stratford has never been slow when it comes to livery embellishments, and No 47170 was apparently five years ahead of its time with the application of large-logo livery. After conversion at Crewe, becoming No 47582, it was outshopped in standard style as BR continued to dither about future livery policy. In autumn 1985 large-logo was given official approval for Class 47s, and Stratford lost no time in returning No 47582 to her proper colours! However, by September 1986 this veteran of the livery game had been chosen to carry Network South-East colours. *(Hugh Dady)*
Praktica IV   50mm Tessar
Kodachrome 64   5 sec, f4

Left: No 45038 in Olive Mount cutting to the east of Edge Hill with the 1205 Liverpool-Scarborough on 29 May 1984. By the end of 1986 the ranks of the 45/0s had been thinned to leave just 19 Tinsley-based survivors working freight traffic. *(John S Whiteley)*
Pentax SP 85mm Takumar Kodachrome 25

Above: No 45077 drifts through the lush Cornish countryside near Coombe with the 1505 Plymouth-Penzance local on 19 June 1985. Under the renumbering scheme this was numerically the last 45/0, but by this date there was little passenger work for a boiler-fitted locomotive. The 'Peaks' have long been associated with the North East-South West route and were the first main line diesel-electrics to penetrate the Western's then hydraulic empire. Initially they rarely ventured west of Bristol and it wasn't until the 1970s that through workings to Devon and Cornwall became common. By 1986 their sphere of operation had receded again and they rarely reached the West Country. *(Hugh Dady)*
Nikkormat FT2 85mm Nikkor
Kodachrome 64 1/500, f4.2

Left: Christmas Eve 1981 finds a lone spectator to watch the passage of *Alycidon* as it climbs past Diggle with the 1350 Liverpool-York. Time was fast running out for the 'Deltics' and this was the penultimate trip that No 55009 would make over the Pennines, an event which had become a regular occurrence for testing the four Class 55s selected for the farewell tours. With just eight days of its BR life ahead there was still plenty of work: trips to King's Cross, Liverpool, Newcastle, employment on the 'Deltic Executive' — the last privately-organised 'Deltic' charter on 27 December — and finally standby duty for the 'Deltic Scotsman Farewell' on 2 January 1982. *Alycidon* was lucky — spared the torch she now enjoys a leisurely existence on the North Yorkshire Moors, lovingly cared for by members of the Deltic Preservation Society along with sister loco No 55019 *Royal Highland Fusilier. (David C Rogers)*
Pentax K1000 50mm Takumar Kodachrome 25 1/250, f2.5

Below: Severe weather not only produces spectacular conditions for photography but often unexpected traction as well. Substituting for an unavailable Type 4, No 31407 struggles to keep time near Greenfield on the steeply-graded route over the Pennines with a late-running Liverpool-Newcastle express. 18 December 1981. *(Robin Lush)*
Nikon FM 85mm Nikkor Kodachrome 25 1/250, f4

No 47541 *The Queen Mother* passes beneath a fine semaphore gantry on the approach to Inverness with a service from Edinburgh on 26 February 1986. During 1986 the area became the subject of a major resignalling scheme which saw track rationalisation and displacement of the old manual signalling. The locomotive carries the Highland Rail insignia depicting a stag on the cabside. *(Brian Denton)*
Nikon FM   105mm Nikkor
Kodachrome 64   1/250, f4.5

Passing Agecroft Junction No 47217 has charge of an up oil train on 10 August 1984. The train is taking the old Lancashire & Yorkshire Railway route from Bolton to Manchester while the diverging line is to Brindle Heath Junction with the L&Y Manchester-Southport/Liverpool lines. The cooling towers belong to Agecroft power station which until 1980 boasted three Robert Stephenson & Hawthorn 0-4-0 saddle tanks, amongst the last working steam locomotives in the Manchester area. (Les Nixon)
Pentax 6 × 7   105mm Takumar   Ektachrome

Kearsley power station sets the scene for a BRC&W Class 104 unit pulling away with a Manchester-Blackburn working on 27 July 1982. In autumn 1982 BR announced a reorganisation of its dmu fleet to reduce the number of units in service. Many three-car units were reduced to two cars and one of the two engines was removed from each power car. The initial trials were carried out on Newton Heath Class 104 sets and were considered sufficiently successful for modification to go ahead of some 450 power cars from the first generation dmu fleet. *(Gavin Morrison)*
Pentax SP1000   50mm Takumar
Kodachrome 25   1/250, f4

The 1128 Chester-Manchester Oxford Road draws to a halt at Lostock Gralam, just east of Northwich, on 15 September 1984. It is formed of a Derby two-car unit, Nos M53942 and M54225. The imposing station building is typical of those to be found on Cheshire Lines Committee routes, often surviving into the present era as private residences. On the horizon is ICI's Winnington works, destination of the well-known limestone trains from Tunstead in the Peak District. *(Paul Shannon)*
Olympus OM10   100mm Zuiko
Kodachrome 64   1/250, f5.6

No 56072 has just crossed the spectacular Harringworth viaduct with a Redland aggregates working on 21 December 1984. The extra installed horsepower and low continuous rating speed (27 km/h) compared to earlier locomotives has proved useful for the movement of block trains. It is interesting that under ideal rail conditions a Class 47 can start heavier trailing loads but is then restricted on gradients by a higher continuous rating speed of 41 km/h. *(John Rudd)*
Mamiya 645   210mm Mamiya
Agfa R100S   1/250, f5.6

Crewe-built No 56131 leads Romanian-built No 56002 near Ryton with a Workington Derwent to BSC Lackenby empty steel carriers working on 14 March 1985. The locomotives were spare due to the miners' strike and would not normally be seen on such traffic. Maintenance economies from the use of brushless alternators in Class 56s have considerably extended the time between routine maintenance when compared with earlier locomotives. (*Peter J Robinson*)
Pentax 6 × 7   105mm Takumar
Ektachrome 200   1/1000, f5.6-6.3

Above: No 08938 in Railfreight livery stands at Eastfield on 9 July 1985. The Highland Terrier proclaims ownership instead of the much-disliked BR corporate symbol. It is pleasing to record that many depots have now adopted symbols, often depicting animals, to proclaim locomotive ownership in preference to the dull shed codes. *(Gavin Morrison)*
Pentax SP1000 50mm Takumar
Kodachrome 25 1/250, f4

Below: One of the spin-offs from steam operation at Marylebone has been the retention of carriage pre-heating unit ADB 968000 (ex-No D8243) seen here with No 08422 on 20 April 1986. Had it not been for conversion of a few members to static carriage heating units, the Class 15s would almost certainly have become extinct, for the last was withdrawn in 1971 at a time when diesel preservation was in its infancy. Sister unit ADB 968001 (ex-No 8233) has now been saved by the South Yorkshire Preservation Society at Chapeltown in Sheffield. *(Hugh Dady)*
Nikkormat FT2 50mm Nikkor
Kodachrome 64 1/250, f4.5

By far the most numerous diesel type on BR, but almost certainly the least photographed, the Class 08 shunter has outlasted all other types. On 19 January 1984 No 08706 shunts local empties near Horbury. *(John S Whiteley)*
Pentax S1a   85mm Takumar
Kodachrome 25

Below: Nos 25057 and 25237 approach Glandovey with the 0744 Shrewsbury-Aberystwyth on 30 June 1984. The trestle bridge carrying the Coast line to Pwllheli over the River Dovey may be seen in the distance. The Class 25s, and before them the 24s, held a virtual monopoly of the locomotive-operated Cambrian services due to their low axle-loading. With the rundown of the class gaining momentum, summer 1984 was to be their last on the Saturdays only holiday trains before Class 37s took over. *(Mike Robinson)*

Pentax ME Super   50mm Takumar
Kodachrome 64   1/500, f4

Right: The last week of November 1982 found No 25326 near Gwernybrenin south of Oswestry returning with loaded ballast from ARC's Blodwel quarry. The branch leaves the Wolverhampton-Chester line at the now-closed Gobowen South signalbox and initially follows the line of the former GWR branch to Oswestry where it picks up the Cambrian main line as far as the site of Llynclys Junction. Until 1984 the working was a job for Chester drivers, but in 1986 it originated from Bescot and was usually in the hands of a Class 31. Traffic on the branch is unpredictable, varying from one train a week to two trains per day, but when the present contract with BR expires in 1988 the line's future will be in doubt.
(Mike Robinson)
Pentax ME Super   50mm Takumar
Kodachrome 64

The onward march of rationalisation has swept away the semaphore signalling at Hunslet Goods Junction, seen here on 14 April 1981 with a short formation HST en route from Derby to Leeds Neville Hill after overhaul. HSTs provide unmatched levels of comfort and reliability for the travelling public, but BR engineers have become increasingly dissatisfied with the performance of the GEC Paxman Valenta engines. Failures reached a peak in the summer of 1983, and in 1985 GEC agreed to pay £7 million in compensation to BR for a variety of defects. At the same time it was announced that four Mirrlees Blackstone MB190 engines would be evaluated to assess suitabilily for a possible re-engining programme. *(Peter W Durham)*
Canon A1   135mm Canon   Kodachrome 64

The adoption of Executive livery, first seen on two Western Region HSTs in the autumn of 1983, seems rather hard to predict. All HSTs and electric locomotives operated by the Inter-City sector seem eligible, but when it comes to diesels confusion reigns. With their 100 mph capability the 50s might have been considered candidates to carry the InterCity flag, but at the time of writing the sector had yet to advertise its ownership. Trying to muscle in on the scene outside Paddington is No 50049 *Monarch* arriving with ECS, while Executive HST Nos 43026/43027 sets out on the 1300 service to Swansea. In a joint anniversary commemorating 400 years of the city of West-minster and the 150th anniversary of the GWR, the HST power cars had just been named *City of Westminster* and *Westminster Abbey* by the Lord Mayor of Westminster and the Dean of Westminster respectively. 29 May 1985. *(Hugh Dady)*
Nikkormat FT2   85mm Nikkor
Kodachrome 64   1/500, f4

Above: The low winter sun picks out No 5097 plodding slowly past a snow-covered Pen-y-gent with a lengthy rake of vacuum-braked coal wagons on 29 November 1969. Certainly one of the more successful first-generation main line diesels, the Derby Sulzers were at one time second only to the Brush Type 4s in numerical strength. Over the years 477 were built in three major batches, the first 151 with the 6LDA28 engine being classified as Class 24, while the later more powerful members became Class 25. Their high route availability made them the most widely travelled of all BR classes, and at one time they were a common sight from Wick to Penzance. *(Gavin Morrison)*
Pentax SP1000 50mm Takumar Kodachrome II

Right: In the early 1950s it looked as if the long-term future of the ex-GCR route between Manchester and Sheffield was assured after large capital investment which included electrification at 1.5 kV dc and building of a new Woodhead Tunnel. However, during the 1960s the line's importance as a passenger carrier declined as BR opted for concentration of block freight over this trans-Pennine route. Passenger services ceased in the first week of 1970, leaving the line to an endless procession of coal traffic and other block freight in the hands of the veteran Bo-Bos. By the late 1970s, with equipment renewal looming, the justification for so many Pennine routes was being questioned. Reduced traffic flow due to deepening recession led to complete closure of the Woodhead route on 20 July 1981. Five months before the axe fell, Nos 76007 and 76026 head east near Torside with coal empties on 10 February 1981. *(David C Rodgers)*
Pentax K1000 50mm Takumar Kodachrome 25 1/250, f3.5

February 1984 saw the somewhat unexpected repaint of No 50007 in Brunswick green, a year ahead of the main GW150 celebration. The Western clearly had ideas about a major renaming exercise for some of its locomotives, with several returning to the old company colours. However, there were differing views in the corridors of power and 1985 saw *Sir Edward Elgar* joined by just four other Brunswick green Type 4 repaints, all Class 47s. Initially the WR was not even allowed to paint its own locos, but after Crewe had failed to select the correct shade of Dulux the remaining three were completed locally at the depots! No 47484 *Isambard Kingdom Brunel* was the only exception — its early grass green livery was painted over at Crewe, and it is seen here in the company of *Sir Edward Elgar* at Old Oak Common on 13 April 1985. *(Hugh Dady)* *Nikkormat FT2 50mm Nikkor Kodachrome 64 1/250, f4.5*

In addition to the five green Type 4s, two dmus were outshopped in chocolate and cream, one single car No L120 in the London division and a Bristol-based three-car unit No B430. It was a livery that the units had never carried, being a copy of the colour scheme originally applied to the Mk1 express passenger stock of the WR in the late 1950s. Inevitably the units proved popular with photographers, and set B430 was frequently to be found on the weekend specials from Temple Meads over the freight-only line to Portishead. The unit is seen here in the cutting at Parson Street on 7 July with the 1210 Bristol-Portishead. *(Ian Gould)*
Pentax 6 × 7
105mm Takumar
Ektachrome EPN 100
1/250, f8

Below: No 37017 leaves Cambridge yard with 8J93, the 1610 Whitemoor-Temple Mills mixed freight on 12 May 1981. The CPV wagons at the head of the formation were conveying cement for the Rugby Portland Cement works at Greenford while the remainder of the train carried steel girders, coal and naval equipment. At this time, all wagonload freight between the North East or East Midlands and London was conveyed via Whitemoor and Cambridge and there were three or four services daily in each direction between Whitemoor and Temple Mills to cater for the traffic. *(Paul Shannon)*
Olympus OM1   50mm Zuiko
Kodachrome 64   1/250, f5.6

Right: No 37067 crosses Lockwood viaduct with coal empties from Elland power station to Clayton West on 4 September 1980. The old Lancashire & Yorkshire branch from Shepley to Clayton West finally closed to all traffic in January 1983. The survival of a passenger service on the branch into the 1980s was probably only due to retention of the line for the coal traffic from Emley Moor colliery near Skelmanthorpe and Park Mill colliery next to Clayton West station. *(David C Rodgers)*
Pentax K1000   50mm Takumar
Kodachrome 25   1/250, f3.2

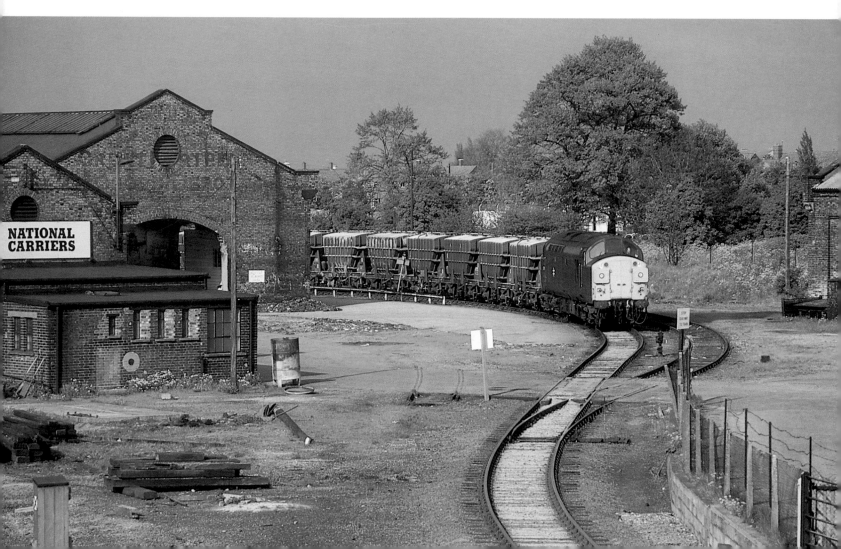

One of the first attempts to find a dmu replacement produced two prototype Class 210 units built by BREL at Derby for evaluation on the Western Region suburban lines. They were very much a diesel version of the Class 317 Bed-Pan units, offering similar levels of comfort. As underfloor engines and mechanical transmission have never been the preferred choice, the Class 210 units had a proper engine compartment and electric transmission similar to the Southern's demus. Unfortunately they were too expensive to produce. Interestingly, the three-car set was powered by a Vee 12 MTU engine, MTU being the company which had absorbed Maybach. The four-car set powered by a six-cylinder Paxman Valenta was caught passing Froxfield bottom lock forming the 0832 Reading-Bedwyn on 8 June 1985. *(Mike Robinson) Pentax ME Super 50mm Takumar Kodachrome 64 1/500, f4*

Introduction of sector-management focused attention on the urgent need for the Provincial Services sector to find replacements for its antique dmu fleet. While most of the first-generation main line diesels had long since been consigned to the scrapyard, their dmu contemporaries were still scuttling around BR's system, often providing a less-than-attractive service. After the extremes represented by the Class 210 and Class 140 railbus a fresh start was made late in 1982, and from this emerged the 150/151 family (see page 12). The first Class 150 production sets were ordered before the prototype had officially been accepted, such was the urgency of the project. Fortunately BREL was able to give the operators what they wanted and within a commendable timescale. On a still summer morning a 'Sprinter' crosses the trestle bridge at Caersws, forming the 0520 Aberystwyth-Shrewsbury. 4 July 1986. *(Mike Robinson)*
Pentax ME Super   50mm Takumar
Kodachrome 64   1/250, f4

Left: Speeding through the hills near Crawford, No 85014 crosses the River Clyde with the 0930 Liverpool-Glasgow on 14 May 1984. (*Hugh Dady*)
Nikkormat FT2   50mm Nikkor
Kodachrome 64   1/500, f4

Above: Motorail services have had a chequered career on British Rail with development of facilities often followed by withdrawal only a few years later. While the concept should be very attractive for holiday travel, the cost has been high, forcing many motorists to grin and bear a long journey on the motorway. On 1 June 1980 No 81012 glides through the Lune Gorge with the 1445 Carlisle-Kensington Olympia Motorail. (*Hugh Dady*)
Praktica IV   50mm Tessar
Kodachrome 64   1/500, f4.5

Above: No 58012 approaches Bardon Hill near Coalville with bitumen tanks from Ellesmere Port on 10 October 1984. That the Class 58s have not lived up to expectation is hardly the best kept secret on BR. Intended as BR's future heavy freight locomotive, they were to be simpler and cheaper to maintain than the 56s. Instead, they have been beset with a string of their own deficiencies and Railfreight management lost no time in making public its disappointment. Haulage ability has been criticised compared with foreign products, and their 80 mph capability simply isn't needed except when they are pressed into emergency InterCity use. *(Robert Osborne)*
Canon AE-1   Kodachrome 64

Right: At the end of the 1960s the CEGB agreed a contract with BR to transport millions of tons of spent fuel ash from its power stations at West Burton, Ratcliffe and Drakelow, to fill worked-out clay pits in the Fletton area south of Peterborough. Merry-go-round trains comprising specially-adapted Presflo pneumatic-discharge wagons are used to transport the ash direct from power station to clay pit. At the unloading plant the ash is pressure-discharged and mixed with water to form a slurry which is used to fill the disused pits. Originally in the hands of Class 47s, the duties have now been taken over by Class 58s. During the 1984 Christmas holiday period, the trains were diagrammed for a pair of 58s in case of failure. Here Nos 58009/016 are about to leave the loop at Fletton with 6E54 from Ratcliffe on 31 December 1984. *(John Rudd)*
Mamiya 645J   80mm Mamiya
Agfa R100S   1/250, f5.6

Below: As the principal route to the far north, it is perhaps surprising that so little daytime freight uses the Highland line. The main Speedlink services run to Dundee and Aberdeen in the east and to Fort William in the west. It was therefore something of a bonus for the photographer to stumble on Nos 20111 and 20064 working a southbound special freight from Inverness over the Findhorn viaduct at Tomatin on 18 May 1984. *(Hugh Dady)*
Nikkormat FT2   50mm Nikkor
Kodachrome 64   1/500, f4

Right: The British answer to the Class 59! No, this is not another haulage record or an emulation of American switcher locomotive practice — just a case of twins to the rescue. On 27 September 1985 No 20082 decided it had done enough for the day and gave up near Shifnal while working a rake of HAA hoppers bound for Ironbridge. A dead sister and train was considered too much for No 20041 and help was summoned in the shape of Nos 20106/

130 borrowed from an empties working. Here the cavalcade approaches Madely Junction, where the train was berthed in a siding to await fresh locomotives. Railfreight has realised the potential of paired Class 20s for many of its short haul circuits, where the higher maximum speed of an expensive Class 58 is unnecessary. *(Hugh Dady)*
Nikkormat FT2   85mm Nikkor
Kodachrome 64   1/500, f4

Above: No 40157 disturbs a bitter winter landscape north of Arbroath with the 1335 Glasgow Queen Street-Aberdeen on 18 February 1978. *(David Moulden)*
Nikkormat FT2   50mm Nikkor
Kodachrome 25   1/500, f5

Right: Probably substituting for a late-running Trans-Pennine service, a Metro-Cammell dmu hurries through a bleak winter landscape at Seamer en route from York to Scarborough. 28 December 1985. *(Les Nixon)*
Pentax 6 × 7   150mm Takumar
Ektachrome 100

The contraction of British Steel has left much of its rolling capacity far from the basic steel production areas, giving BR the opportunity to demonstrate the advantages of block train movement. In recognition of the close links forged between the two industries, five of Thornaby's Class 37s were spruced up for a mass naming ceremony on 30 September 1985 at BSC Lackenby. In addition to sporting the depot motif of a kingfisher, the Thornaby based locomotives were embellished with a white stripe at cantrail level, as opposed to the skirt level stripes pioneered by Eastfield. All five locomotives were named after BSC plants, and this view shows No 37066 *British Steel Workington* and No 37062 *British Steel Corby* passing Cargo Fleet (Middlesbrough) with the 1050 Lackenby-Corby Tubeliner carrying hot rolled steel coil. 7 November 1985. *(Peter J Robinson) Pentax 6 × 7 150mm Takumar Ektachrome 200 1/500, f6.3*

48

In the far west, Railfreight's income is largely provided by the china clay industry. The main mining areas for the Cornish 'white gold' lie to the north of St Austell, and much of the output from the dries is exported by sea from the deep-water harbour at Fowey. This has given an added lease of life to the short branch from Lostwithiel to Carne Point (Fowey), which lost its passenger service back in 1965. Class 37s based at St Blazey handle most of the traffic. On 7 June 1985 Nos 37196/181, both carrying local embellishments of the now-disbanded Cornish Railways, were caught approaching Golant with an afternoon working for Carne Point. A month later No 37196 gained the limelight when it became the first 37 to be repainted in Railfreight livery and was named *Tre Pol and Pen* as part of the GW150 celebrations. No 37181, veteran of the 1965 WR high-speed trials, has since migrated across the Bristol Channel to South Wales. *(Hugh Dady)*
Nikkormat FT2   85mm Nikkor
Kodachrome 64   1/500, f4

Above: May 1986 saw the juice switch-on for the Hastings line, thus bringing to an end the reign of the Class 201/2/3 demus which had worked the route since 1957. The necessity for narrow-bodied stock on this line was a result of skimping by the Victorian contractors during the building of the tunnels. To rectify the deficiencies, additional brick lining had to be inserted, thus reducing the bore. The Hastings units were not AWS-fitted, and in addition their asbestos insulation was considered a safety hazard. BR was anxious to eliminate them and carried out electrification of the line, singling track through the tunnels to allow standard-width stock to pass. On a fine summer afternoon one of the diesel units approaches Etchingham in the Rother valley forming the 0945 Charing Cross-Hastings.
(Andrew Vines)
Bronica ETR-S   150mm Zenzanon
Ektachrome Pro 100   1/125, f11-16

Right: A picture showing the Kent countryside to best advantage and demonstrating that the railway photographer does not have to confine himself to the Settle & Carlisle line to obtain delightful panoramics. On 24 July 1985 a 3D unit, forming an evening empty stock working from Tunbridge Wells West depot, passes Pokehill Farm east of Groombridge during the period following closure when the line remained open for ECS workings.
(Andrew Vines)
Bronica ETR-S   150mm Zenzanon
Ektachrome Pro 100   1/500, f4.5

Left: No 26004 leads No 20126 on the Glasgow Works test train approaching Greenhill Lower Junction at 1215 on 18 April 1986. Despite their age the Class 26s with Crompton Parkinson electrical equipment have outlasted the Scottish Region's other Type 2s, and after extended life overhauls at St Rollox the remaining members look set to see service into the 1990s as Railfreight locomotives. Along with certain Class 20s, they will be the first main line diesels to celebrate 30 years in service.
(Rodney Lissenden)
Pentax 6 × 7
105mm Takumar
Agfa R100S
1/250, f8

Right: At Badicaul just over a mile into her journey, No 26041 heads the 1710 Kyle of Lochalsh-Inverness along the shore of the Inner Sound separating the Island of Skye from the mainland. Introduction of radio signalling was to spell the end for the Class 26s on this and the other Western Highland routes, duties being relinquished to Class 37s. 24 April 1984.
(Mrs D A Robinson)
Pentax 6 × 7
150mm Takumar
Ektachrome EPD
1/500, f8

Above: On 5 December 1983 the 1518 Machynlleth-Barmouth approaches the south end of Barmouth Bridge having just left Morfa Mawddach. *(Mike Robinson)*
Pentax ME Super   50mm Takumar
Ektachrome 200

Right: A Derby-built dmu forming the 1648 Wigan North Western-Liverpool heads towards St Helens at Garswood. 14 February 1981. *(Robert Osborne)*
Canon AE-1   Kodachrome 64

Right: Rows of terraced houses at Chatham form the backdrop for a Class 47 on the 0150 Severn Tunnel Junction-Dover Town Speedlink service on 6 July 1985. The traffic will be shipped across in the train ferry to Dunkerque for onward movement to France, Italy, Spain, Switzerland or Yugoslavia. Until the end of 1986 traffic to other European countries was normally sent via the Harwich-Zeebrugge route. Both routes came under the control of Railfreight International, a separate arm of Railfreight, and the UK ports were served by a comprehensive range of Speedlink services giving overnight access from most parts of the country. Uncertainty throughout the last two decades over the possibility of building a Channel tunnel has given the European business special problems as it grappled with outdated ships and terminal facilities in which nobody was willing to invest. Now that a decision has been reached in favour of a rail-based tunnel it is to be hoped that the flow of international railfreight will increase substantially. *(Andrew Vines)*
Bronica ETR-S 150mm Zenzanon
Ektachrome Pro 100 1/250, f8-11

Left: With empty steel bogies in tow, No 47131 heads north through the Wylye valley near Warminster with a Speedlink service from Eastleigh on 28 May 1985. Freight traffic over this route is extremely variable, with sometimes as little as a single stone train during daylight hours, but on a good day the photographer may be rewarded with a variety of trains in the hands of Class 33s, 37s, 45s, 47s, 56s, and 59s. *(David Moulden)*
Nikkormat FT2 135mm Nikkor
Kodachrome 25 1/500, f2.8

Left: A picture that will surely bring a smile to English Electric enthusiasts. LM-based No 40044 with empty vans for Manchester Red Bank is overtaken by No 55003 *Meld* pulling out of Doncaster with the 0820 Newcastle-King's Cross on 30 May 1978. The Class 40s had pioneered diesel working on the East Coast main line back in 1958 but it was soon realised that their performance was no improvement on the Pacifics which they were to replace. Traffic Manager Gerard Fiennes saw the potential offered by the prototype 'Deltic' and insisted that nothing less than 3000 hp plus would meet future schedules. Despite BTC misgivings over their complexity, a fleet of 22 production 'Deltics' was ordered. Expensive and difficult to maintain they may have been, but until the advent of the HST there was simply no diesel that could catch them. Instrumental in the progressive acceleration of the East Coast timetable, the 'Deltics' will long be remembered as traction engineering at its most exciting. *(John S Whiteley)*
Pentax SP 50mm Takumar Kodachrome 25

Above: On 21 July 1983 No 50028 *Tiger* passes Upper Holloway at 1025 with 9E91 the 0945 Acton-Temple Mills Speedlink service. Most of the traffic had come up from the west overnight, principally from St Blazey, Plymouth Friary, and Exeter Riverside. Some photographs become unrepeatable more quickly than others: since 1983 not only have the signals and box at Upper Holloway been replaced but Acton yard is now closed with traffic diverted to Willesden. As a result visits of Class 50s to East London are now most unusual. *(Hugh Dady)*
Nikkormat FT2 50mm Nikkor
Kodachrome 64 1/250, f5

The introduction of Mk3 sleepers to the Highland routes created a short-term problem in Scotland, for the newly-arrived Class 37s had yet to be converted to 37/4s. The solution lay in redundant Class 25s, three of which were converted to mobile generators and designated ETHEL units. On 1 June 1985 No 37012 *Loch Rannoch* with Ethel 1 (No 97250) pulls away from Bridge of Orchy with the Fort William portion of the previous night's 2100 Euston-Inverness sleeper 'The Royal Highlander'.
(Peter J Robinson)
Pentax 6 × 7
105mm Takumar
Ektachrome EPD
1/500, f6.3

On 24 May 1986 No 37426 *Y Lein Fach/Vale of Rheidol* leads Railfreight loco No 37506 with the 0730 Euston-Pwllheli at Trefri near Penhelig on the Dovey estuary. Both locomotives had emerged from Crewe Works earlier in the year after extended-life overhauls. No 37426 was an eth conversion of 1965-built No D6999 (No 37299) while No 37506 was the new guise for 1961-built No D6707 (No 37007) after dual braking and heavy general overhaul. This Saturdays-only train has provided the first regular loco-hauled service to Pwllheli after Barmouth Bridge was officially reopened to locomotives on 13 April 1986. *(Ken Harris)*
Nikon FM2   50mm Nikkor
Kodachrome 25   1/500, f2.8

Left: Approaching Ely at 0830 on a bitter morning is Metro-Cammell Class 101 unit Nos E50750, E59097, E50191 forming a service from Norwich on 13 January 1981. The signal gantry has since been taken out of use but Ely retained the majority of its semaphore signals as late as 1986 despite the encroachment of the Cambridge area MAS scheme.
(Michael Rhodes)
Canon AE-1   200mm Tamron
Kodachrome 64   1/250, f8

Right: The glorious scenery in Central Wales is evident in this view of Cynghordy viaduct on 11 June 1986. Making slow progress on the climb to Sugar Loaf summit is a Bristol-based Class 118 dmu forming the 1502 Swansea-Shrewsbury. *(Hugh Dady)*
Nikkormat FT2   85mm Nikkor
Kodachrome 64   1/500, f4

The decision early in 1983 to reinstate the pioneer English Electric Type 4 gained universal approval in the enthusiast world. After extensive renovation at Toton, D200 made a celebration run from King's Cross to Carlisle on 31 July 1983, thereafter taking up regular duties on the Carlisle to Leeds run. With the Settle & Carlisle route under threat, this loco provided an irresistible sight for many photographers and travellers alike, but by September its appearances had become less predictable. However with Carlisle Kingmoor responsible for maintenance, D200 was often tried out on the Settle & Carlisle after repairs, and could be found for a few days working out a leisurely existence with the local out and back service to Leeds. On 17 September 1983 it is seen approaching Settle heading for home with the 1635 service from Leeds. *(Robin Lush)*
Nikon F3   135mm Nikkor
Kodachrome 25   1/250, f4

It's all a case of being in the right place at the right time. While the Western attempted to keep a fairly tight rein on its GW150 green 47s during 1985, there were inevitably several outings to foreign parts. No 47628 probably had the most escapes to its credit and is seen at Birkett Common on the Settle & Carlisle with the 1635 Carlisle-Hull on 30 July 1985. By this date the loco had received three green repaints. The original grass green applied at Crewe was quickly painted out at Laira, but being a rush job the result left a little to be desired. With the Paddington opening ceremony to be performed by Sir Robert Gooch, grandson of Sir Daniel, it fell to Old Oak Common to give No 47628 the full treatment in time for the big day on 29 May. Before fitting the cast brass name and number plates the locomotive was completely repainted once again, this time in the correct shade of Brunswick green. *(Les Nixon)*
Pentax 6 × 7   150mm Takumar
Ektachrome 100

Left: The Class 501 units were ordered by the LMR for the London area dc lines with delivery commencing in 1957. A familiar sight on the Watford-Euston and Broad Street-Richmond services, the bars across the drop carriage windows fitted because of the limited clearance of North London line tunnels quickly earned them the name 'Jail' units. The units were maintained at Croxley Green depot; by 1983 they were considered life expired and were replaced by 2-EPB sets and Class 313 units. On 3 April 1982 No 158 crosses the Western Region main line and starts the downhill run towards Acton Central with a Broad Street-Richmond working. *(John Strudwick)*
Praktica LLC   135mm Pentacon
Kodachrome 64   1/250, f8

Right: One of Swindon's last major contracts was a programme of refurbishment for Southern Region emu stock. The 4-CEP units built for the Kent Coast electrification were the first recipients of a facelift that would extend the life of a set by up to 20 years. Only the underframes, bodyshell, bogies and external doors of the original units were reused, but this operation still cost less than half the replacement figure for a new set. When a new London & South East livery was approved by the then sector director David Kirby in 1985, the 4-CEPs were the first units to be treated on the Southern. Emerging from Polhill Tunnel between Knockholt and Dunton Green, No 1521 in brown, orange and beige leads a blue and grey set forming the 1325 Charing Cross-Ramsgate service on 16 March 1986. *(Rodney Lissenden)*
Pentax 6 × 7   150mm Takumar
Agfa R100S   1/500, f4

Left: After several years of buses in advertising livery, it was inevitable that someone would extend the idea to a train. First, and dare we hope last, victim was Class 118 unit No P460 which was repainted at Plymouth Laira early in 1985 decorated with various British Telecom messages: "It's Telecom on the line" and "Making fast connections". Inside, the unit was decked out with display panels describing BT equipment and services. Under the terms of the contract with British Transport Advertising the unit saw service on most of the Devon and Cornish branches through 1985. In this scene P460 is leaving Lipson Junction for Plymouth while engaged on a shuttle service for the Laira open day on 7 September 1985. *(Les Nixon)*
Pentax 6 × 7   105mm Takumar
Ektachrome 100

Above: Another livery to receive mixed reactions was that for Network SouthEast. The striking scheme unveiled by sector director Chris Green on 8 June 1986 brought a touch of colour to the emu fleet, but its application to locomotives seems out of place when those chosen spend just as much time outside the NSE area as in it. On 26 October 1986 No 50026 *Indomitable* arrives at the ex-LSWR Crewkerne station with the 0940 Exeter–Waterloo. Although well within the geographical boundary of Network SouthEast this presents something of a paradox. Wouldn't Network SouthWest have been more appropriate, or were the Southern's planners just keen to regain control of a line which they had partially lost to the WR? *(Ken Harris)*
Nikon FM2   50mm Nikkor
Kodachrome 64   1/500, f4

Above: A major recast of the Scottish timetable in May 1982 saw introduction of a through HST service between London and Inverness. Looking decidedly out of place on the Highland single line, the 0915 Inverness-King's Cross service was photographed at Dalwhinnie on its long journey south. 26 August 1984.

(Les Nixon)
Pentax 6 × 7   150mm Takumar
Ektachrome 100

Right: Led by power car No 43101, which had been named *Edinburgh International Festival*

the previous day, the 1635 (Sun) Edinburgh-King's Cross rounds the curve at Penmanshiel. With so few really fine days that year, it should be no surprise to find that the date is again 26 August 1984! *(Peter J Robinson)*
Pentax 6 × 7   150mm Takumar
Ektachrome 200   1/1000, f5.9

To augment the alternate-hour service from Waterloo to Exeter a stopping service as far as Salisbury was introduced in the 1980 timetable. Some of these workings utilise TC units, but the 1010 Waterloo-Salisbury seen here is formed with Mk1 stock. Providing the power on 12 October 1983 was No 33102, seen approaching Battledown flyover, Basingstoke. *(Ian Gould)*
Mamiya 645 1000S
150mm Mamiya
Agfachrome R100S
1/500, f5.6

The Southern had pioneered high-speed push-pull working with tests beginning in 1962 for the Bournemouth electrification. By 1964-65 enough information had been obtained to authorise conversion of D6580 (which became the prototype 33/1) to operate with modified 4-COR motor coaches and 6-PUL trailers in a formation that was classified 6TC.

After extensive testing, work began at York on building non-powered 3- and 4-TC units, the first arriving on the SR during 1966. At the same time 19 Class 33s were selected for conversion to push-pull operation. Used mainly on the Weymouth-Bournemouth portions of the through London services, the units also find employment on a handful of other workings. On May bank holiday 1985, No 33112 crosses the Kennet & Avon canal near Southcote Junction with the 1408 Portsmouth Harbour-Reading. *(David Moulden)*
Nikkormat FT2   50mm Nikkor
Kodachrome 25   1/500, f3

A Class 47 crosses Eskmeals viaduct with the 1850 Whitehaven-Huddersfield Travelling Post Office on 12 August 1982. Like most of the TPO services, the train has no passenger accommodation but the punctual running of the large network of overnight TPO services is crucial if the Post Office is to deliver 'next day' mail. This service includes a stowage van en route from Workington to Preston for attaching to the Preston-London bag tender. (David C Rodgers)
Pentax MX 50mm Takumar
Kodachrome 25 1/250, f2

From 30 September 1985 'Peaks' were officially barred from working west of Bristol, thus ending an era which had started 16 years earlier when they were drafted into the west to replace North British 'Warships' and other WR diesel-hydraulics. Beating the ban by just three days, No 45046 heads 6B39, the 0550 Severn Tunnel Junction-St Blazey Speedlink service, into the Duchy at Wearde Quay near Saltash on Friday 27 September 1985. During 1985 the three Speedlink trains from Cornwall and their balancing services were all routed to Severn Tunnel and were invariably in the hands of 47s or 45s. Amongst other regular traffic, the services conveyed the products of English China Clay in Tiger Railcar Leasing 80-tonne glw PBA covered hopper wagons (the first and fifth vehicles in this formation) for onward shipment to distribution depots at Cliffe Vale (Stoke-on-Trent) and Mossend.
(Rodney Lissenden)
Pentax 6 × 7
150mm Takumar
Agfa R100S
1/250, f6.3

Right: Unusual power for the 1630 Fort William-Mallaig on 23 June 1982 was No 20191 seen skirting Loch Eilt. With no train heating facilities on the loco, it is to be hoped that such diagramming would only occur in the summer months.
(Mrs D A Robinson)
Pentax 6 × 7   105mm Takumar
Ektachrome EPD   1/500, f5.6

Opposite: Diverted from their normal route via Peak Forest, Nos 20111 and 20165 power a Northwich-Tunsted empties working at Coombs near Chapel-en-le-Frith on 16 June 1985. The Class 20s had taken over the duty from 25s and 45s in 1984, and in 1986 eight members were converted to 20/3s, the work involving modifications to the braking equipment specifically for use with the ICI traffic. The experiment was short-lived and by the end of the year alternative traction had been found for the trains. *(Les Nixon)*
Nikon F   85mm Nikkor   Kodachrome 25
1/250, f4

Left: On 5 August 1986 No 56056 found employment on the 0955 Ardingly-Westbury ARC stone empties seen near Hanging Langford in the Wylye valley. This was the first Class 56 to be constructed with a steel cab structure in preference to the earlier aluminium fabrication, and these later locomotives are recognisable by the larger square grille at the front. *(Ken Harris)*

Yashica TL Electro X   80mm Zeiss
Kodachrome 25   1/500, f2.8

Above: They don't come much cleaner than this! No 56055 leads No 56036 on the approach to Llanwern with iron ore from the docks at Port Talbot on 18 December 1985. At one time these 46-mile circuits were a contender for the heaviest trains on BR, but they have been eclipsed by the Western's aggregate traffic. The second locomotive, which has since been repainted in Railfreight livery, pioneered the large-logo colour scheme when it was experimentally repainted at Stratford in 1978. *(David Moulden)*
Olympus OM1   50mm Zuiko
Kodachrome 25   1/250, f3.5

The 'Gatwick Express' service has certainly brought the Class 73s or 'shoeboxes' out of obscurity. With booming business potential it was decided to replace the tatty 4-VEG units with sets of refurbished Mk2d coaches plus a 73/1 at the country end and redundant 2-HAP cars converted to driving motor luggage vans at the London end. After the launch on 14 May 1984, early problems were experienced with fires caused by arcing, so 73/1s were progressively fitted with flash guards to alleviate this problem. On 16 June 1984 No 73142 *Broadlands* propels a Victoria-bound service through Clapham Junction near the end of its 30-minute journey from Gatwick.
(Geoff Cann)
Mamiya 645J   Fujichrome 50   1/500, f3.5

It now seems hard to believe that No 73142 was not always the Southern's favoured Royal Train Class 73, but after taking part in the ECS working for Lord Mountbatten's funeral train and its subsequent naming, *Broadlands* is very much a favourite at Stewart's Lane. On 6 May 1986 the Royal engagement had particular railway significance because the train was conveying the Queen Mother to open the Hastings-Tonbridge electrification scheme. Climbing Grosvenor bank outside Victoria No 73142, now in Executive livery, has just switched from diesel to electric power. To give a smooth start many drivers tend to prefer using the 600 hp diesel to prevent any jerking caused by gapping over complex trackwork. *(Hugh Dady)*
Nikkormat FT2   85mm Nikkor
Kodachrome 64   1/500, f4

Speeding past Low Gill at 0852 on 19 March 1986 were Derby Research locomotives Nos 97201 *Experiment* and 97403 *Ixion* with 1T21 Carlisle Upperby-Crewe Gresty Lane Tribometer test train. The ageing Class 24 was replaced in 1986 with a Class 31, leaving the Class 46 to continue the tradition of allowing BR locomotive classes nearing extinction to have a last fling as part of the Research Centre's fleet. *(Peter J Robinson) Pentax 6 × 7 150mm Takumar Ektachrome EPD 1/1000, f4.5*

The 20 Park Royal Vehicles two-car sets delivered in 1957 were similar in appearance to the Derby lightweight units, but with a two-panel route indicator and more-rounded windows. Later to become Class 103, the type was always considered non-standard, and body-work problems led to early withdrawals. Some sets have been preserved, and M50396 and M56162 were commandeered by the Railway Technical Centre at Derby to become RDB 975089/90 Lab No 5. The brightly-coloured formation is seen leaving the south portal of Milford Tunnel returning to Derby on 30 May 1985. *(B S Dean)*
Pentax Super A   100mm Pentax
Fujichrome 100   1/500, f5.6

Left: Reliable they may be, but particularly when fitted with eth Class 31s really haven't enough power when it comes to InterCity work. No 31466 would certainly be struggling to keep time with the 1324 Hull-Brighton passing Ambergate on 6 July 1985. The junction is with the old Midland route to Manchester via Peak Forest which is now truncated at Matlock. *(Les Nixon)*
Pentax 6 × 7 150mm Takumar
Ektachrome EPN 1/500, f5.6

Above: On 15 July 1986 No 31252 was entrusted with removing traffic which included NS 1502 (ex-BR No 27000 *Electra*) from the Zeebrugge ferry at Harwich Dock. By the autumn of 1986 Railfreight had announced its intention to close the Harwich-Zeebrugge route and concentrate train ferry operations on Dover-Dunkerque. Despite their age and ponderous appearance, the Class 31s look set to outlast most of their contemporaries. What amounted to major heart surgery during the mid-1960s saw the original Mirrlees engines replaced with conservatively-rated English Electric 12SVTs similar to those in the Class 37s. Despite their low power:weight ratio, they have proved popular on BR with operators and maintenance staff alike. *(Ian Gould)*
Pentax 6 × 7 105mm Takumar
Ektachrome EPN 100 1/125, f11

Right: The railbus story continued to develop after the BR Chief Passenger Manager had sponsored construction of the Class 140 prototype based on LEV (Leyland Experimental Vehicle) technology. Fast off the production line were 20 Class 141 units destined for the West Yorkshire PTE. Passing Horbury Station Junction, a brand new unit is employed on a Huddersfield-Wakefield Westgate service on 2 June 1984. *(John S Whiteley)*
Pentax SP
50mm Takumar
Kodachrome 25
1/250, f4

Left: While cheap to build, the 141s only offered the space of a bus body. Modifications to the jigs enabled BRE-Leyland to offer a full-width body to compete for the second batch of orders for vehicles of this type. These were designated Class 142, and the opportunity was taken to considerably tidy up the front end. The name Railbus was dropped as it was considered down market and in the north the units were christened 'Pacers'. In Greater Manchester PTE red, No 142007 leaves Old-ham Mumps on 8 March 1986 forming the 1230 Shaw-Manchester Victoria.
(Paul Shannon)
Olympus OM1   75-150mm Zuiko zoom
Kodachrome 64   1/250, f6.3

Opposite: The Western had to be different and accordingly called its 142 units 'Skippers'. They received a mixed reaction in the West Country after problems on the tight curves of the Cornish branches and overcrowding during the peak holiday season. On 18 September 1986 Nos 142027/026 pass Hollicombe forming the 1428 Exeter-Paignton.
(Mark Wilkins)
Hasselblad 2000FC   150mm
Ektachrome Pro 100   1/500, f6.3

Left: The Advanced Passenger Train will surely go down in history as another great British 'might have been'. After living in the shadow of the HST, the APT suffered a humiliating introduction after failing in severe weather conditions during its first week of service. Inevitably the media revelled in the misfortune and the train was withdrawn from public view for several months while the problems were sorted out. In the meantime the London Midland appeared to get cold feet about the concept of a fixed-formation train. When the train returned to public evaluation trials, a dark cloud hung over the project, and in 1986 it was finally announced that the APT concept had been shelved and most of the cars were scrapped. On 31 August 1984 No 370007 speeds past South Kenton forming the 1630 Euston-Glasgow relief. *(David Moulden)*
Olympus OM1   50mm Zuiko
Kodachrome 25   1/500, f3.2

Right: No 86238 had achieved nearly two decades of service when the decision was made to name it *European Community*. This was the last Class 86/2 to receive a name and on 6 August 1986 was caught entering Colchester with the 1030 Liverpool Street-Norwich. The Class 86s working on the Great Eastern are serviced at Ilford. Until completion of electrification through to Norwich they could only work as far as Ipswich before handing over to diesel traction. *(Ian Gould)*
Pentax 6 × 7   105mm Takumar
Ektachrome 100   1/250, f8

With the current high cost of repainting a locomotive, observers of the railway scene could be excused for questioning the logic behind selection of engines for repaint. On 12 October 1985 No 47461 *Charles Rennie Mackintosh*, immaculate in a new coat of InterCity livery, sweeps past the old turntable at Hawes Junction and approaches Garsdale with the 1040 Carlisle-Leeds. By the year end however the locomotive's owners had decided that No 47461 should sport the ScotRail legend. At the same time a surprise move saw the red waistband replaced with blue, in line with the standard domestic ScotRail 47/7 livery. *(Peter J Robinson)*
Pentax 6 × 7 150mm Takumar
Ektachrome 200 1/500, f6.3-8

Recently outshopped from Crewe, No 47107 heads 4V73, the 1900 Tyneside-Pengham Freightliner service, round the curve at Stonebridge Durham on 11 June 1986. There is a tendency for enthusiasts to view a large class with a jaundiced eye, especially when they are all outwardly very similar. However, the multitude of new liveries now decorating the class has understandably increased interest in the 47s, which have been described as the bedrock of the main line diesel fleet. *(Peter J Robinson)*
Pentax 6 × 7   105mm Takumar
Ektachrome 200   1/500, f6

Returning to old haunts, No D1015 *Western Champion* proudly occupies the factory once more at Old Oak Common on the evening of 13 September 1985 prior to an open day. Members of the DTG group have spent several hundred hours restoring the 'Mule', a name gained during the long hot summer of 1976. The 'Westerns' will always hold a rather special place in diesel history, for they kindled an interest in railway enthusiasts which had lain dormant since the end of steam. By the time they finally departed from BR, interest was at fever pitch with tour after tour sold out. Had it not been for the Class 52s one can but wonder whether today's enthusiasm for modern traction would be so great: even as late as October 1975, a very novel trip taking a 'Deltic' to Cardiff for the first time created such indifference that it ran half empty! *(Hugh Dady)*
Nikkormat FT2   50mm Nikkor
Kodachrome 64   1 sec, f4

As the end approached for the 'Deltics', it was no great surprise when the Eastern announced a programme of farewell tours for which selected locomotives would be specially groomed. Those not chosen were left to soldier on with any major fault bringing almost certain withdrawal. On 28 October 1981 No 55008 *The Green Howards* had just escaped the axe after running around for several days on one power unit. A decision had been made to give this locomotive a transplant at Stratford, and meanwhile it was undergoing a boiler test at York before working down to London. Although the ER headquarters at York had always been the centre of 'Deltic' administration, it was only after the class had been displaced from top link duties that the depot there received an allocation. Soon after withdrawal of the 'Deltics' the depot was closed and today is used as an annex to the National Railway Museum. *(Hugh Dady)*
Praktica IV   50mm Tessar
Kodachrome 64   5 sec, f4

Above: The British portion of the Venice-Simplon-Orient-Express operated by Sea Containers Limited has found considerable extra use since its introduction on luxury charter traffic and day excursions. For the 1986 season the successful 'Beaulieu Belle', was extended to become the 'Bournemouth Belle', although it continued to run to Poole for stock servicing as had been the case in previous years. In June 1986 No 33008 *Eastleigh*, the last 33/0 to be given a general overhaul, was turned out in Brunswick green, and the VSOE Pullmans became a favourite working. On 14 June 1986 the locomotive skirts Southampton Water at Totton with the 1035 ex-Waterloo working. Within a fortnight, a white waistband and red buffer beams had been added, and by mid-August No 33008 had been further embellished with white cab window surrounds. Still not satisfied, further modifications were carried out in October bringing the scheme as near to the authentic mid-1960s livery as was practical given the nameplates and TOPS numbering. *(Ken Harris)*
Yashica TL Electro X 80mm Zeiss
Kodachrome 25 1/500, f2.8

Right: In May 1985 the private Great Western & Scottish Railway Company launched a series of luxury tours based upon three-day cycles of the West Highland routes. The train is called 'The Royal Scotsman' and the vehicles used are finished in Caledonian livery. On 30 May 1985 participants were treated to a view of the Highlands at their best as No 37183 climbed towards Achallader, north of Bridge of Orchy, on the Oban-Fort William leg of the tour.
(Les Nixon)
Nikon F 50mm Nikkor Kodachrome 25
1/250, f4

No 37033 approaches Werrington Junction, Peterborough with the 1855 Skegness-Cambridge on Sunday 27 July 1975.

(Colin Ding)

Rolleiflex 80mm Planar   Agfa CT18
1/250, f2.8